Yellow Umbrella Books are published by Capstone Press
151 Good Counsel Drive, P.O. Box 669, Mankato, Minnesota 56002
www.capstonepress.com

Library of Congress Cataloging-in-Publication Data
Bauer, David (David S.)
    Adding arctic animals / by David Bauer.
    p. cm.
    Summary: Simple text and photographs introduce the animals of the Arctic, grouped to provide practice in solving easy addition problems.
    ISBN 0-7368-2913-X (hardcover)—ISBN 0-7368-2872-9 (softcover)
    1. Addition—Juvenile literature. 2. Zoology—Arctic regions—Juvenile literature.
[1. Addition. 2. Zoology—Arctic regions.] I. Title.
QA115.B38 2004
513.2'11—dc21
                                                        2003010973

Editorial Credits
Editorial Director: Mary Lindeen
Editor: Jennifer VanVoorst
Photo Researcher: Wanda Winch
Developer: Raindrop Publishing

Photo Credits
Cover: Joel Simon/DigitalVision; Title Page: Creatas; Page 2: Joel Simon/DigitalVision; Page 3: EyeWire; Page 4: Gerry Ellis/DigitalVision; Page 5: Creatas; Page 6: Jim Brandenburg/Minden Pictures; Page 7: Jim Brandenburg/Minden Pictures; Page 8: Corel; Page 9: Lynn M. Stone/Bruce Coleman, Inc.; Page 10: Jim Brandenburg/Minden Pictures; Page 11: Creatas; Page 12: Erwin and Peggy Bauer; Page 13: Erwin and Peggy Bauer; Page 14: Creatas; Page 15: Creatas; Page 16: Royalty-Free/Corbis

Adding Arctic Animals

by David Bauer

Consultants: David Olson, Director of Undergraduate Studies, and Tamara Olson, Ph.D., Associate Professor, Department of Mathematical Sciences, Michigan Technological University

Yellow Umbrella Books

an imprint of Capstone Press
Mankato, Minnesota

The Arctic is a cold place.
Yet many animals live here.

Let's add arctic animals!
How many can we find?

One polar bear looks for food.

Two others play nearby.
Add the polar bears: 1 + 2 = 3

Arctic hares have white fur
in winter.

They have brown fur in summer.
Add the arctic hares: 2 + 2 = 4

Some wolves live in the Arctic.

Foxes live here, too. Add
the arctic animals: 1 + 2 = 3

Female caribou live with their babies.

Male caribou often live alone.
Add the caribou: 3 + 1 = 4

Musk oxen live in herds.

They huddle together for safety. Add the musk oxen: 3 + 6 = 9

Harp seals swim in the
cold water.

They come on shore to have babies. Add the harp seals:
6 + 2 = 8

The Arctic is full of animals!
Add them up!

Words to Know/Index

Word Count: 120
Early-Intervention Level: 10